Interview with Mr. Kevin Rohm

Aaron Elson

The BiblioGov Project is an effort to expand awareness of the public documents and records of the U.S. Government via print publications. In broadening the public understanding of government and its work, an enlightened democracy can grow and prosper. Ranging from historic Congressional Bills to the most recent Budget of the United States Government, the BiblioGov Project spans a wealth of government information. These works are now made available through an environmentally friendly, print-on-demand basis, using only what is necessary to meet the required demands of an interested public. We invite you to learn of the records of the U.S. Government, heightening the knowledge and debate that can lead from such publications.

Included are the following Collections:

Budget of The United States Government	Code of Federal Regulations
Presidential Documents	Congressional Documents
United States Code	Economic Indicators
Education Reports from ERIC	Federal Register
GAO Reports	Government Manuals
History of Bills	House Journal
House Rules and Manual	Privacy act Issuances
Public and Private Laws	Statutes at Large

US Army Sustainment Command

Interview with
Mr. Kevin Rohm

Abstract

In 2003, the Army Field Support Command (AFSC) and the Joint Munitions Command (JMC), collocated at Rock Island Arsenal, Illinois, began a comprehensive oral history project aimed at chronicling a full-spectrum slice of the commands' role in Operation Iraqi Freedom, Operation Enduring Freedom and the Global War on Terrorism (GWOT) broadly defined. Because the command was over 90 percent Department of the Army (DA) civilians and heavily augmented by contractors, the command realized by 2003 that they were managing the largest ever deployment of DA civilians and contractors into a combat area, and so, over 150 interviews were conducted focusing on the GWOT-related experiences of DA civilian members of the two commands during 2003 and 2004. Starting at the same time, Mr. George Eaton, currently command historian at US Army Sustainment Command (ASC), has conducted to date almost 200 more interviews with DA civilians, contractors and uniformed military personnel. This oral history project aims at delivering an overall picture of the activities and duties of the various components of AFSC and JMC and their combined efforts to support the Army's worldwide operations. The interviews look at growing trends in areas of both success and concern, while also accounting for how logistics support commands have completely transformed operational- and strategic-level logistics since 2003. ASC personnel are forward deployed at every forward operating base in Iraq, Afghanistan, Kuwait, Qatar and Djibouti, among others. Indeed, what began as a small operation in 2003 has become a robust organization, globally deployed, and is now a key player in all four of the Army's materiel imperatives; to sustain, transform, reset and prepare. The following interview with Mr. Kevin Rohm, a supply management specialist/logistics assistance representative (LAR), covers such topics as being deployed to Iraq, the CONUS Replacement Center, LARs during Desert Shield/Desert Storm, LARs during Iraqi Freedom, working conditions in Iraq, living conditions in Iraq, being wounded during a mortar attack, DA civilian wounded and the medical treatment of wounded DA civilians.

Interview with Mr. Kevin Rohm

25 May 2004

JV: My name is Jannette Voss (JV) and it's Tuesday, 25 May 2004. Aaron Elson (AE) and I will be interviewing Mr. Kevin Rohm (KR).

AE: Hi, Kevin, how are you?

KR: I'm fine.

AE: My name is Aaron Elson. I'm an independent historian working with Janette and George Eaton on the project they're doing. Before we begin the interview I'm going to read you a short release statement, so please listen carefully. If you have any questions, feel free to ask, okay? The information gathered during this interview is for historical research purposes and may be used by other nongovernmental researchers. Before its final release you'll have an opportunity to review the final transcript. Do you understand and agree to have your transcript released to and/or used by nongovernmental persons? If you answer no, the interview will still be done, but it will be marked "Not for Release."

KR: Yes, I understand. I'll accept.

AE: Thank you very much. Now tell me your job title before you were deployed?

KR: I actually carry two job titles. The official one is supply management specialist, and they call us logistics assistance representatives or LARs.

AE: You're a supply management specialist and a LAR. I've heard the term LAR a few times. Were you considered emergency essential or did you volunteer for deployment?

KR: No, I was emergency essential. I was notified of my call forward in August, just before I deployed to Korea for an exercise.

AE: Oh, so you were preparing to deploy for Korea, but you instead went to Kuwait?

KR: No, I went to Korea, and when I got back I went to Iraq.

AE: Now, this was this past August?

KR: Yes.

AE: How long have you been working as a Department of the Army civilian?

KR: Since 1980.

AE: Were you active military before that?

KR: Yes, I was. I served from June 1973 to June 1976, active duty.

AE: How did you become a supply management specialist?

KR: I've basically been in supply ever since I was in the Army. In the Army I was a supply clerk; an armorer. When I got out, I was in a lot of varied positions, all of them having something similar to do with logistics. When I went to work for the government in 1980 I took a job with the Weapons Registry, and afterwards I became an item manager for the M-155 Sheridan. Then I entered the Army's supply-management intern program down at Red River Army Depot, and I've been climbing the ladder in the supply field ever since.

AE: You said that you have two separate job titles. How did that come about?

KR: Well, a LAR is not an official title. We're logistics management specialists, we're equipment engineers, or we're supply management specialists, one of those three official job titles. All of us are called LARs.

AE: Did you go to Kuwait after Korea, or did you go directly from Korea?

KR: I came back from Korea. I spent a few weeks in my new home that my wife bought while I was in Korea. I'd actually been transferred here in June and we were still living in temporary housing at the time that I was notified and went to Korea, and also at the time that I was notified for Iraq. So I spent about, I'd say, a month in my new house and then I deployed through the CONUS replacement center (CRC) at Fort Bliss, Texas. I arrived there on 12 October and departed there on 18 October, and flew through Chicago to Frankfurt, where I then took a military hop to Baghdad.

AE: What was your experience like at Fort Bliss?

KR: It felt a little bit like basic training again all over. We basically slept in our usual beds, which is the same kind of bed that a trainee gets. We had the wool blanket, the standard pillow that doesn't really prop up your head well. Let's see, what else about it? Foot lockers, wall lockers. Yeah, it was going back to basic.

AE: Now, what about the procedures, the shots and the meals? Were they efficient?

KR: They were run like any other Army organization would run things. They were rather efficient. I thought they were done well.

AE: Were there many people going through the CRC at that time?

KR: I believe there were approximately 160 people processing that week. I could be wrong about that number. It could be more.

AE: Is that a mix of civilians and active military and contractors?

KR: And Reservists, and some of them were even something else, which I don't think I can say.

AE: Did you go to Kuwait, to Camp Arifjan?

KR: I never touched Kuwait.

AE: You went straight to Iraq?

KR: I went straight to Baghdad.

AE: And what did you go there as?

KR: As an LAR. My assignment was support of the 2nd Armored Cav Regiment out at Muleskinner, which was on the southeast corner of Baghdad.

AE: When you got the notice that you were going to deploy to Iraq, did you have any trepidation when you saw in the media how things were going over there?

KR: No, I had no trepidations. I had no fear. This is not my first deployment.

AE: Is it your first deployment to, I guess, what would be considered a combat zone?

KR: No.

AE: Where had you been before?

KR: Operation Desert Shield/Desert Storm. I was a LAR with the 7th Corps at that point.

AE: And how would you compare the two?

KR: One was a war, one was a guerilla action.

AE: This one would be the guerilla action?

KR: Yes, exactly.

AE: Could you describe it a little more, from your experience?

KR: Well, Operation Desert Storm, we had a clear objective. We accomplished that objective quite swiftly, and once we had control there were no further repercussions. In this war, we didn't really gain control, although we became superior, but now the enemy is fighting us from under the rocks, behind the bushes, around the corner. He's the gentleman standing in the crowd who I can't see. He's the unfamiliar face that none of us know. He's the person standing next to us. It's just a totally different war. This is, from what I understand, from friends who have been to Vietnam, very similar to Vietnam in that regard, in that there was no safe place in Vietnam. You were attacked in Saigon. You were attacked everywhere and that's what we have here. There are no fronts. There's no line of defense. The enemy is there, sneaking around behind you and there's no real defense against him.

AE: When you arrived at Camp Muleskinner, what were your specific duties?

KR: My specific duties were to investigate the causes for what we call not-mission-capable supply, in other words the absence of parts to repair the equipment that supports the 2nd Armored Cav Regiment, and to find plausible solutions and expedite that material into theater.

AE: When you say plausible solutions, can you give me an example of a problem and a solution?

KR: A problem would be that the item manager is out of stock and is not expecting to get anything in for a year. An alternative, plausible solution to that then is to go to an assembly line at Anniston Army Depot, for example, where they repair tanks, and pull the part that I need off of the assembly line, and get that shipped as an alternative.

AE: Just like that?

KR: Yes. We're empowered with that ability. We have the knowledge of a number of alternatives that we can take in any given action, and we're also empowered to make a direct contact call to the people who can make it happen.

AE: So the item manager is somebody back in CONUS?

KR: The item manager is somebody at what's called national inventory control points, who controls the stock, the usual procurement, storage and issue of items.

AE: What specific types of equipment did you work with?

KR: Everything that the Army owns. There are no specifics.

AE: From what I've seen and heard, the biggest problem - in terms of supply - was the up-armored Humvees. Did you deal with that?

KR: Yes, quite often. We had a lot of engine failures.

AE: Engine failures?

KR: That was the majority of what I had seen. I don't know the specific cause. What they were doing was they were switching out engines and we were running short on them.

AE: Who would switch the engines? Were these contractors?

KR: No, the engines would be worked on by the soldiers. They'd pull the engine and they'd replace it.

AE: They'd remove the engine and put in a new one?

KR: Now understand, I'm not maintenance. It would be a maintenance guy who'd be able to speak more specifically to the question.

AE: The reason I ask is I guess the image one has is that the biggest problem with the Humvees was these improvised explosive devices (IEDs). This is the first I've heard that the engines were having problems.

KR: Well, there were a number of jeeps that were damaged or destroyed by the improvised explosive devices that were planted alongside the road.

AE: Was the sand a problem, or the dust?

KR: I couldn't tell you what was wrong with the engine. I have no knowledge of the specific problems leading to the failure that would cause the unit to have to pull the engine and turn it in for a new one. I'm simply the guy who enables them to get the new ones when they're difficult to get.

AE: I understand. But just to elaborate a little bit more. The engine would fail. The soldiers would remove the engine and you'd get them a new engine?

KR: In this case, because they were in short supply and the item manager was protecting his safety levels. I had to make a phone call to, more or less, gain the release of the items.

AE: Okay. That brings me to another thing. The expertise and the knowledge of the civilian workforce from Joint Munitions Command (JMC) and the Army Field Support Command (AFSC) - these positions, the LAR positions, require a lot of experience and expertise and with new people coming in, how do the newer people acquire this knowledge? There are a lot of retirements taking place, or will be in the next few years. Are the skill sets being replaced? If somebody comes in to replace you, is there a risk they won't know the right people to call, or the right things to do?

KR: We make sure they don't, that they have everything they need to do their job. We give them lists, contacts. They basically learn more from doing than anything else. Plus, they have the ability to reach out and touch any LAR who can give them guidance as to what their steps should be. So, we have the worldwide network of LARs as a backup for the new person.

AE: You stayed pretty much at Camp Muleskinner, or did you travel much?

KR: I traveled. I stayed one week, when I first arrived, at Baghdad International Airport, right there at our log assistance office at Baghdad International Airport. Then they transferred me. I flew by UH-60 from what they call BIAP, Baghdad International Airport, to Muleskinner, which was on the opposite side of Baghdad. I was at Muleskinner for approximately three weeks and the colonel had to pull his logistics management specialist person, his readiness LAR, out of another camp called Dogwood and he still had to backfill that position, so he started looking for somebody who could do it. I volunteered to go in place of the logistics management specialist that was at Dogwood, Sue Moynihan. She was the LMS there at Muleskinner with me. For the colonel it was a choice between her or myself and I openly volunteered, more or less because Sue already had things well in hand there at Muleskinner. I think she needed to stay at Muleskinner, and I had also been told that Dogwood was a dangerous situation, that they were being mortared almost on a daily basis, two or three a night, and I felt I was better suited to that kind of stress and environment.

AE: When you arrived there, what were your specific duties, again?

KR: I was acting at that point as the LNO, liaison officer, between Colonel Hodges, the LSC commander, or LAO commander, and the 1st Armored Division, Division Support Command (DISCOM), which was located there at Dogwood. I had under my control the multimedia communications set, the two contractors who operated it, and also there with me was the DLA representative. He's kind of like a LAR for the Defense Logistics Agency. There was also a Tactical Army Command (TACOM) LAR there as well, Carol – I can't remember it right now. We evacuated her probably about seven days into my being there. She went back to the Baghdad International Airport, where she stayed at the LSE there, in a better environment.

AE: Oh, was there a reason why she was evacuated?

KR: The living conditions at Dogwood were primitive. We had outhouses for going to the bathroom. The showers were towers, water tanks and sprayers that you basically got in and got a cold shower with. The food they were serving was out of T-ration trays. We're not talking freshly cooked meals here. And then also, the mortar fire, the almost daily attacks from somebody, it was rather unnerving, and a few of the people had gotten to the end of their rope. That's why I was brought in. That's why we got Carol out of there, because they were reaching the point of maximum stress.

AE: It sounds very, very stressful. The food, was that the MREs?

KR: No, meals ready to eat, that's what we usually had for lunch. As far as I know, they served one hot meal that wasn't an MRE, and they used what they call T-rations. T-ration is a ration the government came up with. You heat it up in its metal pan, and then you open it, and I think each pan serves 20 people, so you don't have to have anybody cook up a meal. They just heat it up and cut it open and then spoon it out to the folks.

AE: Oh, okay. How would they clean up? Did you have like mess kits, like in the Army, or do they have paper utensils?

KR: Actually, it was paper trays, paper compartmented trays, plastic silverware and paper cups. So it was all thrown away.

AE: And there was no way of getting food from the local economy? I mean, was it a sealed-off camp?

KR: No. We're still talking Dogwood?

AE: Yes.

KR: Yeah, actually, Dogwood was on a metal-fabrication outfit that was somewhere out there. From what I understand, part of the camp there was used as a training camp for the new Iraqi Army, and it wasn't connected to any town. In fact, this was about 25 miles southwest of Baghdad.

AE: Tell me more about the mortar attacks. Janette had said that you were wounded over there?

KR: Yes, I was. On the day I arrived, 16 November. It was the first day they hadn't actually had a mortar attack in quite a while. They'd been getting a couple of them shot at every night. The shots were random. They weren't aimed. It was just like harassment fire. When I arrived on the 16th, it stopped and it stopped for nine days. On my tenth day there, 25 November, I got up around 6:00 or 7:00 o'clock. I checked my e-mails. Then, at around 9:00 o'clock I took a walk over to the motor pool. I needed to get a tire for my vehicle, so I made arrangements to have that installed on the vehicle the very next day. We had an up-armored Humvee. I got to the maintenance shop. Nobody there. I started walking around looking for them and found them in a tent. There was a comedy troupe there doing stand-up comedy in the recreation tent and that's where I found the maintenance crew. I had to wait through the show, enjoyed it immensely, too. I can't recall the names of the individuals. One of them has his own show, apparently, I think it's on the WB. But anyway, they were all good. I do remember they were all good. Then after it broke up, the troops went back to their jobs. I went over to the maintenance office, made my arrangements for that tire change for the following day, went back to my office, did my work. I was researching parts and stuff. Around 6:00 o'clock I started putting together kind of the day's events, readiness information and stuff, and I was getting ready to go over to what was called the battle update briefing that evening. That would've been held at 7:30 p.m. that evening. I had gone over, gotten my evening meal at the mess hall, and had come back. I had just eaten it. It was around 6:30 in the evening, and while I was sitting there at the desk we heard the first round come in. It was real close. I recall yelling out at everyone to get their helmet and flak vest on. Actually we had interceptor vests, not flak vests. I turned around. Mine was lying on a cot behind my chair, at my desk. So I grabbed my vest. I put it on. And it must have been as I was putting my helmet on, given the way the shrapnel hit me, that the second round hit the roof of the building we were in. We had actually tents set up. They were frame tents set up inside of a great big warehouse. The warehouse had concrete sides and a corrugated-steel roof, supported by I-beams. The mortar round had apparently hit the I-beam almost straight above our location, slightly, I would say, 15 feet from my location, straight over, which was directly over the location of our two contractors who operate - our two Tamsco contractors. They were spared, basically, because the I-beam, the way the mortar hit, hit directly on the I-beam so that none of the shrapnel from it could come straight down on that. I think they would have gotten the brunt of it had it come all the way through, and the I-beam not been there. I was hit in the stomach by two large chunks, and also the arm. I didn't know that I had even been hit. After that one, I yelled out, let's get the, you know, Hades out of here, proceeded to stand up so that I could start moving to a bunker. Actually, it wasn't a bunker we were going to head to. I should say it was the up-armored Humvee. From what I understand, these guys in past mortar drops had used the up-armored Humvee as kind of a bunker. About the only thing it couldn't defend against would be a direct hit. As I started to get up - I don't think my butt got more than six inches off the chair - I felt something kind of ooze from my stomach, I looked down and I saw myself gushing out. So I realized I was hit. I yelled out, I'm hit! About that time, I heard somebody else say that they were hit. It was Don Evans with the Defense Logistics Agency. He'd been - according to the reports I read after the fact, apparently been laying down at the time that the mortar attack began, and he got hit just as he was getting out of bed. Took one through his leg. I guess he had a lot of cuts and stuff around his head, his neck, his chest.

AE: Because you were inside the building, did you hear it coming, the way that –

KR: No, we didn't hear the plunk sound that you usually hear with a mortar round. I imagine that's probably because they were probably shooting at us from as far away as four kilometers.

AE: Now once you realized you were hit, then what happened? What was the medical treatment like?

KR: The medical treatment, actually, I'd have to say it was quick. I fell backwards when I realized I was hit, and also felt that I couldn't really get up like I thought I was going to, and when I did I kicked my feet up and onto the cot that was behind my chair to more or less treat myself for shock. Gerald Stevenson, he was one of the Tamsco contractors, started running out of the tent and through the building, screaming, "Medic, medic!" He came back shortly and started to try to look after me. We were still being shelled at the time, so I consider his actions rather heroic, or maybe even foolish, I don't know which. Since it was done for my and the other guy's health, I'd have to call it heroic. But anyway, the medics were probably within two or three minutes after him. They cut off my bulletproof vest. They put one of the field dressings on my stomach and tied it. I'm overweight, so I can imagine that was a problem in itself.

AE: Well you know, maybe that was also a blessing. In terms of a stomach wound.

KR: You never know. One of the pieces went as deep as five inches and was laying along my back near my spine when they removed it. The other one made a one-and-a-half-inch-deep hole. It had to have gone through my flak vest in order to make the hole where it did. And the shrapnel itself couldn't be found anywhere. It had apparently ejected itself after it made that hole. I've heard of stranger things.

AE: You describe the vest as not being a bulletproof vest, but as an interceptor vest?

KR: It's called an interceptor. It's actually supposed to be better than the flak vest. It's supposed to be a bulletproof vest. But there are also supposed to be small arms protective insert (SAPI) plates that are inserted in this, titanium plates that are supposed to give you maximum protection from rifle fire and mortar fire. From what I understand, when a mortar blows up, the shrapnel travels at high velocity, the same kind of velocity that you find in a high-powered rifle. And without the SAPI plates, the vest does not give you full protection from shrapnel. It only gives you partial protection.

AE: Now, you're in the supply business and the logistics business. I've heard before that there were not enough of these SAPI plates to go around. Could you maybe talk a little bit about were you supposed to have had those?

KR: Yes, I was. Everybody who went into the theater, into Iraq, was supposed to have them. It was on my issue list when I went through the CRC at Fort Bliss. The only size they had available was small, and I'm a extra-large, myself. When we got there, the LSEs had what was called second chance vests. These are bulletproof vests that cops usually wear underneath their uniforms. We wore those as a substitute until we received a shipment of these interceptors. They'd gotten sizes up through large. I know I looked for an extra-large but couldn't find one, which would have been the proper size for me. So I took a large instead. When I asked about the SAPI plates, SAPI plates did not come with the issue of the vest in this case. Apparently they were out of stock as well. So, a bulletproof vest without a SAPI plate is a flak vest, so that's better than nothing at all. So I took it, and that's what I wore to Dogwood.

AE: After that round, how many more rounds came in? Do you know?

KR: My own estimate is 15 to 20. And I was hit with the second one.

AE: Boy, I can hardly imagine the stress...

KR: All of them landed in close proximity to our building. Only one of them actually hit the building. But the rest of them were so close, I mean, the sounds were just horrifying. When I fell backwards I lost my helmet, and I couldn't reach it, so what I tried to do was scoot myself across the floor until I could get my head up against this metal water cooler that was near my desk. I was hoping that that would give me enough protection, that and the three-quarter-inch plywood around my sleeping enclosure. I was hoping that would give me enough protection if another one had hit the building. Fortunately, none ever did.

AE: What thoughts raced through your mind the moment you knew you were hit?

KR: First thought was, my wife is going to be pissed.

AE: Pissed?

KR: Yeah. Mad at me for getting myself in such a fix, because I told her, "Yes, honey, I know it's dangerous, but don't worry, I won't do anything stupid." Obviously, going there was the stupid thing that I'd done. The next thought through my head was that this was it, this was how I was going to die, because I had known many friends who served in Vietnam who got hit in the gut and that was it for them. A gut wound is supposedly one of the worst you can get and I had two great big ones down there. So as I lay there bleeding out I'm saying, "I'm dead." This is it. This is how it's going to be for me. And I accepted it. I thought to myself that this is a good death. It was in service to my country. I didn't die as an old man on my couch, having nothing to tell the world, you know, having lived my life quietly. So, I thought it was a good death. I accepted it. I was ready to go.

AE: Do you have children?

KR: Yes, I do.

AE: And did you think about them?

KR: No. My children are 31, 30 and 27.

AE: They're grown. The reason I ask is I'm thinking of the old line from General Patton about how the people who served under him would be able to put their grandchildren on their knee and tell them that they fought with George S. Patton and didn't shovel shit in Fort Polk, Louisiana. Do you have grandchildren?

KR: Yes, I do. I have one currently and my oldest daughter is about to give birth to my second grandson.

AE: Oh, congratulations.

KR: Thank you. I found out about her being pregnant while I was at Dogwood.

AE: So that was a very eventful period. In those ten days, what sort of things did you do? What problems did you encounter and what solutions did you come up with?

KR: Oh, I don't even want to go there. It was too numerous to enumerate for you.

AE: Does one stand out that you could use as an example?

KR: No. No. No, there were literally hundreds of problems to resolve, and most of them were basically routine. They follow along the lines of what I've already described to you.

AE: Well, one thing that I've come across in these interviews, an issue I guess you could say, is that the Army wants to format operations, whereas a lot of things are dependent on individuals that the Army would like to replace - if one LAR leaves then another LAR comes in, everything should still proceed as planned. But a lot of individuals who took initiative, or had ideas which were not in the textbook, so to speak, made a big difference. Did you see that happening?

KR: Oh, we've had LARs take their own initiative and come up with some fantastic solutions to many problems. Some of them were just our own personal problems. When we were at Muleskinner, we had the problem of trying to give ourselves a little luxury in a very austere environment. When we couldn't get any water for bathing, our guys actually went and tapped into a pipe. They went and scrounged water pipe from other locations. Some of it was even gas pipe. They assembled a feed line all the way over to our building, where we could get more than just a trickle of water. That's just one of many cases. Let's see - trying to think of some other times while we're talking ingenious fixes. I've seen them in a lot of other different operations as well. I'm just trying to remember something here that I can actually tell you. A lot of this stuff is classified.

AE: Okay, you don't need to go into that. Where do you see things going, in terms of the civilian workforce over in Iraq?

KR: Well, I don't see it going away. The things we do are very essential to the government, essential to the success of the Army. They can't have a soldier do it. The soldier just doesn't have the kind of logistics background and experience that the civilians have to begin with, let alone the connections and everything that we have, and the authority that we're given as well. I don't see the situation improving over there, either. We have ourselves a real guerilla war, and it'll be there for as long as we're there. We have too many enemies in the world that this puts us out there where they can reach and touch us, and gives them a target to shoot at. And so long as we stay in Iraq, we stay that. And those people will continue to go after us. I believe a lot of this is Al Qaeda. A lot of this is just basically Muslims, or people of the Muslim world, who have always hated what the United States represents or stands for and have come there thinking that they're helping Muslims by attacking us. And a lot of it is basically what's left over from Saddam Hussein's rag-tag Republican Guard, the Mujahideen fighters that he also had, those things.

AE: Given the danger level, is it going to be more difficult to get people to volunteer for deployment?

KR: Oh, I'm certain that's already affected the volunteer element of it. Now my job in it is not volunteer. This is actually what LARs are supposed to do. It's a requirement. So when they tag you and say you've got to go, you've got to go. It's either that or quit the job. For the other positions that go over there, there are staff positions, I believe, that are used at Balad, at logistics support element (LSE) Iraq, and then there are staff positions at Kuwait and Saudi Arabia as well. But the ones in Iraq, I imagine, are extremely hard to fill with volunteers, given that people are being killed left and right.

AE: Now one thing they've been doing when they can't get volunteers, and don't have emergency-essential people, is replacing some positions with contractors. Do you see that happening? I know it's difficult with a LAR to bring in a contractor, but I think it's been done.

KR: Personally, I've never seen it happen, so I can't vouch that that's what's being done. I know that a lot of times they'll try to find military personnel or reservist to replace them. That's been the only experience that I know - in fact, the current operations tempo that we're at is unprecedented. We've never been at war in two different places at the same time. In fact, actually, if you consider the operations in Bosnia and Kosovo also actions of war, right now we're in four different locations with a significant force, five if you count Korea, which is actually a cease-fire. Our forces are right now spread extremely thin and so are our civilian resources. And because our civilian resources have been spread so thin, we've actually gone out to the Reserve Component. A young lady from San Antonio, she's a Reserve major, has volunteered to work as an LAR, and I forget which force that she's currently serving with over there, that we actually had to go out and get a non-logistics assistance representative to be a logistics assistance representative, speaks to our need to have more civilians in this program, let alone the others. We're certainly understaffed.

AE: Are they bringing in new people?

KR: I'm seeing new Reserve officers being brought in to act as LAOs, or LSE commanders, and I'm seeing Reservists being brought in to act as LARs.

AE: When you were at Camp Dogwood, even though you were there a short period, how many hours a day would you put in working?

KR: I would get up around 6:00 or 7:00, no alarm clock, nobody would wake me up. It's just whenever I woke up. Get up. I'd put my shirt on, my pants on, and I'd slip on my thongs for the first couple of hours of the day, get a cup of coffee, sit down at my desk, check and see what new e-mails I had. Then I'd take a look at the new 026 reports and I'd start investigating all the cataloguing information, stock availabilities, etc., using our various sources of information. About two hours later I'd probably get up, put my boots on and I'd take a short walk to kind of - oh, - decompress from that. I'd come back about 10, 15 minutes later, get back on the computer, and I'd basically work like that, on and off several hours, taking a 10-15 minute breaks every two or three hours, until around midnight, when I would turn off my computer and get in bed and go back to sleep.

AE: So that's like an 18-hour day, 19 hours?

KR: Actually, considering my sleep pattern, 18-hour days.

AE: Who would you communicate with mostly back in the States?

KR: We have LARs who sit at the national inventory-control points, John Carver at TACOM here at Rock Island, John Wakefield at TACOM in Detroit. Tony Runyon at CECOM, Communications Electronics Command. There was a Cedric Green down at the Aviation and Missile Command (AMCOM), at Huntsville, Alabama. Those are the Army national inventory-control points. Also, John Reynolds was at one of the DLA activities. For a short period of my deployment he actually ended up following me into Baghdad and became the supply LAR there at the LAO 1st Armored Division at the Baghdad International Airport LAO. So we kind of lost his assistance at that point. But he had contacts there that we could then use. Plus, I had the DLA rep sitting there next to me, so I didn't really have to use them, if you would. I'd just hand my problems to him, the DLA person, that is.

AE: And how were the communications back with Stateside?

KR: Exceptional. I've been doing this for 20 years, well, most of the 20 years, anyway. When I deployed to Southwest Asia, our telecommunications was using a field phone, which was very poor, very difficult. We had basically the same problems the soldiers had. By the end of Desert Storm they came up with the satellite phones. There were three different models. One of them offered voice and electronic computer communications. One of them was voice alone, and the other one was computer alone. So, that was a big step up and we're talking 1991. When I was deployed to Bosnia in 1996, January '96, we had the new flyaway packages. These were a concept cooked out of the Desert Storm experience. It included a 10-foot satellite dish, a switchboard with 100 phone lines that had their switch at Fort Monmouth, New Jersey. We bounced off of satellites into Fort Monmouth, and then we were able to make government, military DSN phone calls from that switch at Fort Monmouth. So it was real time. It was real easy. We had along with that some mobile phones, that had a 25-mile range that we could also tie into that - when we weren't with a hard-line capability. That was a real nice flyaway package. I liked that. Now we have the current, what we call a multimedia communications system, an MMCS, and that's operated by Tamsco. That's using more or less the same 10-foot dish, only this has Internet network capabilities, telecommunications capabilities. It's the envy of every general officer, when they see the capabilities that we have for communications, and in fact, I think this time it got me in trouble. The reason why our operation was still there was because the general did not want to rely on the signal capabilities that he had been given by his signal company. He wanted our communications, and that's why we had that little office there, was to support him and his staff.

AE: Now this is a personal question, but were you right about your wife being pissed?

KR: No.

AE: How did she react when she learned...

KR: When she found out that I had been hit, she accepted it. We have a philosophy that you just can't change what's already happened and you just go with the flow. And she went with the flow real well, from what I understand. When I got home she smothered me with love, and totally convinced me that I had actually died and gone to heaven, because there was no way in hell this was my wife. She was treating me too well.

AE: Oh, that's wonderful. How did she learn of your injuries?

KR: My wife works here on the island. She works for the Tank Automotive Command. In fact, she actually works for the office that supports the TACOM LARs. So not only is she a LAR's wife, but she was also working with LARs. From what I understand, they worked hard to keep it from her. My command sent several people over to her boss's office, where they closed the door, had a short discussion and had the chaplain waiting outside, I guess. Then they called her in, and if they needed the chaplain they were going to call him in after that. They sat her down and they told her we've got bad news. It's not that Kevin's dead or anything, but he's been injured. And then they proceeded to tell her what they knew. At the time, what they knew was not the right story, but that's okay.

AE: What story did they give her?

KR: The casualty report out of Baghdad they'd finally gotten said that I had superficial wounds and that I was returned to duty. So what they told her was simply that it wasn't serious or anything, but I was wounded by a mortar round and that I would be okay, and that they were just cleaning up the wounds and they were going to send me back to work. That was actually the report on Don Evans, not myself. Don had superficial wounds here and there. His worst was one piece of shrapnel that went all the way through the calf muscle of his - I think it was his right leg, if I remember the pictures correctly.

AE: Was anybody else wounded in the attack?

KR: No, just him and myself.

AE: In other mortar attacks on the base, was anyone killed?

KR: I was never informed of anybody in the past being injured. I can't say that that's a fact, per se. But I was never told that anybody else was ever injured in any of the attacks.

AE: Where were you taken for treatment?

KR: We had just stood up an aid station there on the base. They took me first to the aid station. They cut all my clothes off at the aid station. The unit chaplain was standing next to me and I was cracking jokes with him and the medical staff as they were getting me prepped to go. I understand they gave me a morphine feed, and then they wrapped me in a blanket. I was completely naked underneath that, strapped me to the stretcher that I was on, and hooked something to the side of it for my IV, and then they loaded myself and Don into a helicopter that had just arrived. They flew us from Dogwood to the Green Zone, where the 28th Combat Support Hospital was in operation. They took us in immediately. I recall the doctor telling me what they were going to do, explaining absolutely everything to me that he could about what he was about to do and what my condition was. And then the next thing I recall was waking up and him standing over me telling me that everything was a success, that he removed four feet of my intestine, that some of the shrapnel was still in my arm, but they cleaned up most of it, and not too much else. I've seen that doctor again. I understand his name is Major Ponder and I saw him on television. He was the one examining Saddam Hussein after he was captured.

AE: Really?

KR: Yes. I recognized the bald head. Let's see. They operated on me about 11:00 that same night, on the 25th. They medically evacuated (MEDEVAC'd) me the following day about 4:00. They took me by helicopter from the Green Zone to Baghdad International Airport, into a tent where I waited for the C-141 to arrive, pick us up and take us back to Landstuhl. It was about a five-hour flight. I was kind of in and out during the flight, so I really don't have much recollection of the flight. And then they got us to Landstuhl. I think it was about 2:00 or 3:00 in the morning, Thanksgiving Day. This would have been the 27th. My Thanksgiving turkey came to me intravenously. I wasn't able to eat for -- I think it took me three days before my bowels began to move again.

AE: And when did you come back to Rock Island?

KR: It was on the 2nd of December. Significance here is that the 2nd of December was also my wife's birthday.

AE: When did you go back to work?

KR: I went back to work on January 5th.

AE: What is it that you're doing now?

KR: What I did before deployment. They have me working, training - LAR training, what we call the Logistics Assistance Program, Operations Course and Senior Managers Course. I don't teach the courses, mind you. What I do is drum up students for these classes that we give six times a year, and then I seek funding for the class to get them there, pay for their motel, pay for their transportation. I coordinate it all. I get everything done between them and the money folks, so that everybody's happy here. It has absolutely nothing to do with being a supply management specialist. We'll put it that way.

AE: Several of the people I've interviewed had issues in receiving proper pay, with all the hazardous-duty pay, being overseas, and the combat zone, etc., etc. With you having been wounded, were there any problems in getting paid properly?

KR: Actually, none. I think they had me improperly listed before anyway. You know what the Fair Labor Standards Act is? Fair Labor Standards Act is a law that basically tells the private industry that when an employee works over 40 a week, they're supposed to be paid time and a half and double time for holidays. Government does not have to abide by that law. In fact, most government employees are called exempt from the FLSA coverage. For some odd reason, when I went to Iraq, at first I was not exempt and I was being paid time and a half for all my overtime, which started a whole flurry of questions when people found out how much money I was getting, because they just couldn't believe the amount. The government corrected that mistake later, and I ended up getting the regular flat time that everybody else was getting. We were working basically 88 hours every two weeks of overtime, and getting paid the same as when we worked regular hours. For me that's a beef. I think when government enacts a law, the government should live by the law, and they should not be allowed to be exempt from it, but that's just my opinion. That's telling me that I'm really not worth what somebody else working in the private industry is worth. That's what it tells me. We don't get any compensation. They tell us that, well, we're only going to pay you for 12 hours a day. It doesn't matter that you're working 18 hours a day. You can only be paid for 12 hours a day. That's the maximum money that we can give you. And that's usually how they pay. If I'm working an 18-hour day, I expect to be paid for an 18-hour day. I would if I worked for a private industry. So, I have issues with that. But that's been challenged in the past by other people, Desert Storm, and from what I understand, the system finds for the government in all those cases, because government has an exclusive right to violate our civil rights, so to speak.

AE: Why can't they offer you compensatory time, because they don't have enough people to fill in?

KR: No, they don't offer us compensatory time. I've never been offered compensatory time in lieu of the other. Basically because they'd have to do it officially, and under the rules of compensatory time, if it isn't used in six months it converts to pay, and then I'd end up getting paid for the hours beyond the 12 that I was told I couldn't be paid for. So that's why they wouldn't offer it. Interesting. We also have pay caps. As I understand it, if all of my pay, which includes not just regular pay, the overtime, but also the hazardous-duty pay, post differential, all the added things to our pay that we get when we deploy, if that exceeds the pay of a Congressman, our pay stops. They can no longer pay us for the rest of the year, because we're capped by law. So once you hit that point, that magic number, you really can't work - everything you do is for free, beyond that. I'm a GS-12, step 10. I'm at the high end of my pay cap. I make about $73,000 a year without war. So, it's very easy for me to hit that pay cap.

AE: The pay cap is what, around 125?

KR: I think it's around there, somewhere around there, 130,000 or 135,000, if I'm not mistaken.

AE: That sounds like a lot, but it's really not that much...

KR: Not when you consider that these people are working 18-hour days for six months.

AE: Especially with the skills they bring in compared to private industry.

KR: Exactly. I wouldn't go there saying that their skills are greater. Their skills are different. Their skills are geared for the government, whereas private industry is geared for private industry. There's a big difference between government and private industry in this kind of action and operation.

AE: Except that they're contracting out more and more things to private industry. Do you have a take on that?

KR: There are a lot of things going to contractors, and from what I understand, a lot of the stuff that LARs used to do has gone to the contractors, so the contractors own the maintenance on these newly procured systems, the new helicopters and stuff. So the LAR has less to do as far as teaching the soldier how to fix the equipment, and more to do with acting as a contracting officer rep. But that's only in that arena. I have not seen that in TACOM, CECOM and in my own position.

AE: I think I've asked about everything I wanted to ask. Are there any observations you'd like to make? Anything pressing, or anything you think ought to be included? Anything I should've asked but didn't know to?

KR: I can't think of anything else. You've pretty much covered the gamut.

AE: How are you treated by your co-workers now? You know, even though there've been over 3,000 Americans - these are, I think, mainly military, but over 3,000 people wounded, not too many of the civilian workers have been wounded in combat like that.

KR: To my knowledge there have only been two other Department of Army civilians who have been wounded, myself and another gentleman by the name of Tom Ironside, who works for the Communications Electronics Command at Fort Monmouth. I believe he's currently stationed in Germany. The other gentleman, of course, is the one who got blown up with me. He's the Defense Logistics Agency Representative, and I believe Don is out of Dayton, Ohio, if I remember correctly. The rest of the civilian deaths that were over there, or civilian injuries, are contractors, and though they're contractors, they're still contracted with the United States government, which makes them or their injuries equivalent to ours, for recognition.

AE: But how do your co-workers treat you? Do they treat you with deference? Do they look up to you as being battle-wounded?

KR: It's something of a mix. There are those who are jealous of the honors I've received. There are those who are in awe. There are those who look up to me as somebody with a vast experience they'd like to possess, probably not the experience of the explosion itself, but it's made them more aware that I'm there, that I've been around for a long time. It's made others, especially those with a military past, very respectful. My cousin was also over there in Iraq. In fact, he's supposed to still be in Iraq. He got a purple heart out of this action himself. He was wounded. He's a soldier with the 94th Field Artillery, 1st Armored Division. I looked him up while I was over there. We spent a day or two together. He was wounded in an action where they were trying to control a crowd. One gentleman decided to become forceful and aggressive, took a brick, flung it, hit my cousin in the face, taking out several teeth, ripping his face apart. The gentleman is dead, from what I understand. They ended up killing him. But my cousin got a Purple Heart for the wounds.

AE: And a lot of plastic surgery, I would imagine.

KR: They did a good job stitching up his lip, and all he needs now are some false teeth to replace the ones he lost. But I guess he's in good spirits.

AE: Well, that's good. Now, when you say you were joking with the doctors, do you remember any of the banter that...

KR: I cannot remember half the things - I like puns, and I like metaphorical jokes, so it was probably along that line.

AE: That kind of spirit is not uncommon when people are wounded like that.

KR: My wife was actually told that I was cracking jokes all the way through. And she said, "That's good. I know he's okay now."

AE: All right, I think that covers pretty much everything. I appreciate your having taken part in this. When the transcript is ready Janette will get in touch with you and you can go over it.

AE: Okay, it was good talking with you. Bye.

KR: All right, bye-bye.

END OF INTERVIEW

CPSIA information can be obtained
at www.ICGtesting.com
Printed in the USA
BVHW011116121220
595501BV00016B/30